The 21 Emotions of a Willowing Girl

Aurora Howlett

BookLeaf Publishing

India | USA | UK

Presentation by *BookLeaf Publishing*

Web: www.bookleafpub.com

E-mail: info@bookleafpub.com

ISBN : 9789357447188

First edition 2021

DEDICATION

This book is dedicated to Mrs. Leblanc, my grade 7 and 8 English teacher who first introduced me to the power of poetry.

ACKNOWLEDGEMENT

Huge shout out to BookLeaf Publishing for this opportunity, it's always been my dream to publish a book. I also want to say thank you to all of my English teachers who have helped me on my writing journey. No thanks to any of my brothers who interrupt me when I'm trying to write and won't leave me alone no matter what I do. Thanks to all the adults in my life who support me and encourage me to keep writing. Thanks to all the bookstores and cafés that inspired many of these poems. And thanks to anyone that buys this book, you all mean so much to me!

PREFACE

Listen, I'm a nerd. I read books for fun and watch anime, and now I'm publishing a book. I mean, I never thought I would be so invested in fictional things, but here I am, overly invested in fictional things. It came as a surprise to no one that I was writing a book, except for me. So after countless days thinking of moments in my life and countless nights putting words together, I am finally publishing this book!

Content

The wind is swirling with a beautiful glow
I see the flowers dancing
Deep in thought of far off places
A feel of never-ending

Twisting flowers in dancing rain
Drops of dew in meadows
Fall asleep in strawberry bushes
And wake in earthly glue

Lakes, lily pads, and lilac bushes
Painted in my mind
Dreams of swirling pixy dust
Falling into my pride

The darkness stretches around me like wet paint
flowing
The stars flashing their most brilliant grin
The quiet sound like a hundred bees buzzing
As I watch the empty world spin

Unsure

My smiles are real
So why am I so scared when they come
If smiles mean happy
Then fake ones mean what?

I love my pain
Because at least she doesn't leave me

When will my mind learn
That my heart has a mind of its own

When my day comes
I won't hate you for pulling the plug
Only sit
Thinking of the life I never lived

Extravagant

Pop and grind and shouting stories
Car Windows open wide
Full of cocky extravagance
I can never die
Years fade as I watch the sky
Pinks bloom into orange
Wonderful is the different
Don't you wish you'd known it

Blue

Chill wind on ice
Frozen eyes showing nothing new
Skates around this darkened track
Painting murals for all to view
Crystal flowers made of snow
Cold stems forever froze
Pain made all so numb
Chill wind killed us young

Dangerous

Beware the women who show themselves
Who do what they want to do
These women show the world no kindness
As they build it up a new
Beware the women who laugh and scream
Who live their lives as they want too
These women are dangerous
But that is nothing new
Beware the men that cry and knit
Who aren't afraid to laugh
These men have fought so much to be
Comfortable at last
Beware the quiet child
Sitting in the back room
They hold within the secrets of earth
Contain the will of all that birth
Beware the ones with love in their eyes
The ones with broken soles
They've seen great pain
And yet,
They choose to let it go

Depression

How can I live like this?
The tears on my check that I can't cry
The hate in my heart I can't say
The brake in my bones,
For someone else's game
The poison in my blood sinking in
The collapse in my brain
The dark comes in from the sky
As the pain comes into my mind
The char and black
The smoke and fumes
The burning mind of my darkest days

Misty

Lilac, greens, and silver trees
She's painted in the stars
Looking on the world her own
Seeing love herself in the dark
Tall walls covered in vine
Darkest viridescent
Brick shows behind it all
Brighter even then her stars

Denial

Freezing clouds blowing freezing rain
I stand at the stop
Looking at pictures of sunny days

Acceptance

After rain there is a rainbow
After night there is a day
She bows her head
Then stands up tall
And learns to love it all
Bright lights follow me home
Blinding blue and yellow
As I fall asleep
New places old tombs
I see the distance
And I want to go there
So one day
One day far away
I will be there
I will be part of that light
Be happy

Anticipation

Want, struggle, need
What do I truly need?
Will the wait become fate
And will I need that which I wait
If I need to wait all day
For months or years
Then I can say
That which I wait
I can acclimate
If I decide to listen to fate

Freedom

The little things
Or so I'm told,
Are the things
We look back at the most
So come with me
For a picnic
Camp or hike
Let's run in fields
And live our lives
With little things
In mind
I want to float
I want to soar above the world
And leave my problems behind
I want to be above everyone
And see the world
In its true form
I want to touch the sky
And then disappear
I don't want to be seen
I want to hide up in the sky
With the birds
And the sun

Fear

Stares, eyes
bewitched lies
Follow, drown me out
Feel their blaring gaze
On hidden places
Banned from them
Place I hide
Never looking
Me in the eye
Hold my breath
And tears come out
Fallen eyes
Only doubts

Memory

Strange husk and magic lamps
Coffee grinds within my hands
Walls full, antique designs
Morning sips and kind goodbyes
A magic shop right in my eyes
Broke cups on the walls
Cans from old places still
Top shelf peace
And gentle will

Hate

The cold of hate
The heat of passion
Lost brothers
Never to be found
Hate is only as bright as light
And I am burning
Standing in a spotlight
The dark is seen to the side
So stroke the fire
To keep it live

Dread

Pills and bottles
Everyday
But they help take my sad away
Swallow whole
And choke them down
I wish I didn't need them around
For the rest of my life
I'll take these pills
To feel alright

Heartbroken

Her cold hands find my cheeks
As she breathes out one last time
Come, my love, come
Join me in my frost and cold
With trees of gold
And ground of snow
Live a life of lies
And fireflies
As we watch the empty world grow

Safe

Sleep
Hush
I'll protect you
I'll keep the demons gone
I'll use my sword
My words my shield
And my strength increase
With every minute of sleep
So hush, let it all go
The dark won't hurt you
When I am here
And I am

Sins

Tall as mountains
Fierce as night
The bright moon is the only thing in sight
You stand tall, over the hill
But grave pain Awaits you still

Want want want
The pig eats all
You set insight
And as do you,
With blank delight

The warmth of whole
The fire lit
The bedroom marked with a candlestick
It's you to crave
But Hell do find
Those who spend all their time

For years of work
I get respect
And Holy water
That disinfects
But you stand high
Above the hill
I want your kingdom
Oh so filled

The man outside
Is in need of help
The lord has said to give it out
But I won't give in
To such little things
As feeding those
Who I don't forgive

God will not be
In me heart
His love is fake
As are his Brothers
They lie to steal
The broken Hirth
I will not let them take my own

Sweet love

Soft and sweet
like caramel
She melts into my lips
As if she always belonged to me
As if she held
sunshine on her tongue
And she held me as if
I was her universe
Sunshine, Mist
And other stuff,
Like dandelions
And teddy bear fluff
Happiness comes
When I think of you
Forever in motion
A moment away

Escapism

Hide behind broken bars
Candlesticks and rusty old cars
Sheltered by my favorite books
Myths and stories
That almost exist
Feelings don't erase
But they can be replaced
With those from others
From a distant place

The smell of rain and drops of ink
On precious paper
Painted white or gold
Or silver brown
I miss their smell and windy nights
Pages flipping
It's my delight

I miss the feel
Of dry and warm
Of cold concrete
On the floor
Pillow forts
Lands of comfort
I want to go back
To the worlds I preferred

Spring breeze
And buttercups
My books turn
With honey fluff
Green grass
And silver brass
A day okay
Without winters way

Melancholy

Lemon pulp and cinnamon
Spice and auburn brew
Dandelions turned to dust
And weep as flowers do
A train bench
Red or blue
Tired faces that smile through
Home comes with that bench
And coffee taste of auburn scent

www.ingramcontent.com/pod-product-compliance
Lightning Source LLC
La Vergne TN
LVHW021353200726
843509LV00014B/2827